Out in Space

by David Conrad

Content and Reading Adviser: Joan Stewart
Educational Consultant/Literacy Specialist
New York Public Schools

COMPASS POINT BOOKS

Minneapolis, Minnesota

Compass Point Books
3722 West 50th Street, #115
Minneapolis, MN 55410

Visit Compass Point Books on the Internet at *www.compasspointbooks.com*
or e-mail your request to *custserv@compasspointbooks.com*

Photographs ©:
PhotoDisc, cover, pp. 1–24 (background); Visuals Unlimited/Mark A. Schneider, 5; PhotoDisc, 6, 7 (aurora borealis, meteor shower); PictureQuest, 7 (hubble telescope, international space station, space shuttle, satellite); ArtExplosion, 7 (jumbo jet); Visuals Unlimited/John D. Cunningham, 8; Visuals Unlimited/Dell R. Foute, 9; Comstock, 10; PhotoDisc, 11; NASA, 12 (*Sputnik*, dog); PictureQuest, 12 (rocket), 13 (NASA astronauts, space shuttle); PhotoDisc, 13 (space walk, human on moon, space station), 14; PictureQuest, 15; PhotoDisc, 16, 17; PictureQuest, 19; PhotoDisc, 20, 21.

Project Manager: Rebecca Weber McEwen
Editor: Jennifer Waters
Photo Researcher: Jennifer Waters
Photo Selectors: Rebecca Weber McEwen and Jennifer Waters
Designer: Mary Walker Foley

Library of Congress Cataloging-in-Publication Data

Conrad, David.
  Out in space / by David Conrad.
     p. cm. -- (Spyglass books)
Includes bibliographical references and index.
  ISBN 0-7565-0242-X
  1. Astronomy--Juvenile literature. [1. Astronomy.] I. Title. II.
Series.
  QB46 .C77 2002
  520--dc21
                        2001007318

Contents

Looking Up

Long ago, people made up stories about groups of stars that made them think of their gods.

The Greeks named many of these groups of stars.
Today many people still call the stars by these names.

Big Dipper

Fun Fact

Sometimes people named groups of stars after things found in their daily lives.

Where Earth Ends

Earth is covered with a thick blanket of gas. At the top of this layer, almost 200 miles (322 kilometers) above the ground, space begins.

Earth

How Far from Earth?

Hubble Space
Telescope
372 miles (600 km)

International
Space Station
260 miles (420 km)

Space Shuttle
124–372 miles
(200–600 km)

Satellite
186 miles (300 km)

Aurora Borealis
50–100 miles
(80–160 km)

Meteor Shower
50 miles (80 km)

Jumbo Jet
6 miles (10 km)

Watching and Learning

Before people could travel
into space, they had to learn
a lot about it.
In space, there is no air
for people to breathe,
and no food or water
to keep them alive.

Fun Fact

Observatories have roofs
that slide open when people use
their giant *telescopes*.

Scientists had to study
the skies carefully to learn
about any risks, and
to think of good *solutions*.

Fun Fact

Nearly 400 years ago,
Galileo Galilei used
two eyeglass lenses
to make the first telescope
to study the skies.

First Flights

Before sending people into space, scientists sent *satellites* into the sky on rockets. These satellites *orbit* Earth, and send back important information.

Space Time Line

| 1957 First satellite (*Sputnik*) | 1958 First animal in space | 1961 First human in space |

1965	1969	1971	1977
First space walk	First human on the moon	First space station	First space shuttle

The Moon

One of the great moments of space exploration happened in 1969. As millions of people watched on their televisions, Neil Armstrong took the first steps on the moon.

Fun Fact

There is no air on the moon, and no wind, so Neil Armstrong's footprint is still there.

The Solar System

After landing on the moon, people wanted to know more about the solar system. They have sent **probes** to study the sun. They have also sent many probes to Mars.

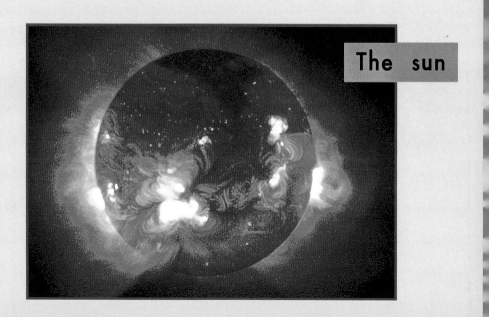

The sun

Mars

Good Neighbor

Mars is the planet closest to Earth.
Scientists have sent many probes
to it to search for signs of life.

Far, Far Away

Scientists also study the stars and planets with powerful telescopes such as the Hubble Space Telescope. The Hubble floats in space above Earth.

Maybe someday people will explore these areas in person.

Hubble Space Telescope

Fun Fact

Some telescopes search for sounds of other life that scientists are not yet able to see.

Space Art

1. Mercury is the hottest planet in the solar system.
Draw a creature that might come from such a hot place.

Mercury

2. Mars is the planet that is most like Earth, but it is cold and dry. Draw a creature that might live on Mars.

Mars

Glossary

observatory—a special building where scientists can study space

orbit—to travel around an object in space

probe—a small spacecraft that sends information back to Earth

satellite—something that travels around an object in space

solution—a way to solve a problem

telescope—a tool that makes faraway objects, such as stars and planets, seem closer and larger

Learn More

Books

Branley, Franklyn M. *Floating in Space*. New York: HarperCollins, 1998.

Fowler, Allan. *Stars in the Sky*. New York: Children's Press, 1996.

Mitton, Tony, and Ant Parker. *Roaring Rockets*. New York: Kingfisher, 1997.

Web Sites

Brain Pop

www.brainpop.com/science/seeall.weml (click on "solar system," "moon")

Kidzone Fun Facts for Kids

www.kidzone.ws/planets/index.htm

Science Monster

www.sciencemonster.com

Index

GR: I
Word Count: 224

From David Conrad

I am a scientist who lives in Colorado. I like to climb mountains, square dance, and play with my pet frog, Clyde.